[SURVIVING THE IMPOSSIBLE]

SURVIVING IN A WORLD WITHOUT POWER

CHARLIE OGDEN

THE SECRET BOOK COMPANY

©2018
The Secret Book Company
King's Lynn
Norfolk PE30 4LS

ISBN: 978-1-912171-04-0

All rights reserved
Printed in Malaysia

Written by:
Charlie Ogden

Edited by:
Kirsty Holmes

Designed by:
Danielle Jones

A catalogue record for this book is available from the British Library.

CONTENTS

Page 4	The Lights Go Out
Page 6	Evil or Accident?
Page 10	Finding Your Friends and Family
Page 14	Dangers in the Dark
Page 16	Choosing Your Hideout
Page 20	Gathering Supplies
Page 24	Life Without Power
Page 26	Making Your Own Electricity
Page 30	Surviving in a World Without Power
Page 31	Glossary
Page 32	Index

Words that look like THIS can be found in the glossary on page 31.

THE LIGHTS GO OUT

It's the final scene of the movie. The hero is just about to corner the baddie after an out-of-control car chase... then the screen goes black. The power's gone out! However, never knowing how the film ends will be the least of your worries when you realise this isn't any ordinary power cut; it's a worldwide blackout! Living in a world without power may force you to become a real-life hero, fighting to survive. We use electricity every day, sometimes without even thinking about it. The **REFRIGERATORS** that keep our food cold, the heating that keeps us warm, the lights in our houses – none of these would work in a world without power. When the power goes out, you're going to need all your brains and courage to get somewhere safe, warm and supplied. Without power, people will still panic. Frightened, panicking people can be more dangerous than the power loss itself.

With no news on TV, no computers and no internet, it will be hard to find out why the world has lost power. There is one thing you can be sure of, though. Whether the world loses power due to electricity cables breaking, at the hands of an evil genius or simply because too many people decided to make a cup of tea at the same time, everyone will find out that there's no power at the same time. This means that your only **ADVANTAGE** could be that you've made a plan and can act quickly.

EVIL OR ACCIDENT?

EMP WEAPONS

Knowing why the world is without power could save your skin, as well as help you work out whether the power will ever come back. If things have gone really badly, an evil genius might have cut off the world's electricity with his newest Electromagnetic Pulse device. An EMP is a piece of technology that sends out a huge blast of **MAGNETIC ENERGY**, which destroys all the electronics in its range. If this has happened, expect to see planes falling out of the sky, prison gates flying open and out-of-control cars on the motorway. When you see this **DESTRUCTION**, you'd better start running. The world is in some serious danger and you won't want to be caught up in the madness.

SOLAR FLARES

Mad geniuses armed with EMP devices aren't the only way the world could be left without power. Giant explosions in space can also affect the power supply on Earth. The Sun can release a huge amount of energy at any time in a blast called a **SOLAR FLARE**. If the energy from a solar flare reached the Earth, it could destroy all the electronics – just like an EMP device.

Fact: In 2012, a giant blast of energy from the Sun narrowly missed the Earth. We were lucky that time – but if it had hit us, we could have all been plunged into a world without power.

HACKERS

Some people who know a lot about computers are able to gain access to all kinds of things – government computers, top secret information, you name it. These people are called 'hackers'. Once someone has gained entry to the right computer, they can steal or change the information that is stored there – or even shut the whole thing down.

THE GRID

We use a system of power stations, **PYLONS** and wires to send electricity all over the world. All of these together are known as the electrical grid. For power to stop working in one area, all that needs to happen is for one of these wires to break. You can think of this like a row of dominoes – one falls and knocks the next one over, which then knocks down the next. However, if one domino is removed the whole thing stops.

If there's just one break in the electrical grid, power can usually be restored. However, if lots of wires break at the same time – which could be caused by a **SURGE** of electricity – it would be a lot harder to fix. The grid would not be able to carry electricity to where it needed to be, leaving us all without power.

Top Tip: NEVER try to fix a broken wire yourself. You could hurt yourself very seriously. Don't touch wires, especially if you see any exposed metal; this could give you a painful or even deadly shock!

SMOKE SIGNALS

Long before we had mobile phones, Native Americans used smoke signals to talk to people far away. Making a smoke signal involved covering a fire with a wet blanket for a couple of seconds, then taking it off to allow a puff of smoke to rise into the air. The smoke puffs could be seen for miles and could help people to tell their friends if they were in danger. You probably won't be able to have a detailed conversation using smoke signals, but you can use fire and smoke to show people where you are. You just have to be careful not to give away your position to the wrong people — and to not set your blanket on fire.

Fact: Different **TRIBES** of Native Americans used smoke signals in different ways. This meant they could send up smoke signals that anyone could see, but only people from their tribe would know what it meant.

SECRET HIDEOUT

SIGNS

If you have to leave in a hurry, the easiest way to tell your friends and family where you have gone is by leaving a clear sign. This could be as simple as leaving a note pinned to your bedroom door or drawing an arrow on the ground with your name underneath it.

Top Tip: Once you have managed to meet up with your friends and family, it's best to move on... before anyone else finds you.

DANGERS IN THE DARK

In a world without power, you're going to need to be brave. The everyday heroes that used to keep you safe, such as police officers and firefighters, will no longer be able to do their jobs. A lot of the technology they relied on – such as computers, radios, police cars, ambulances and fire trucks – might no longer work. With no power left to light up the streets, some people may use the darkness to sneak around and steal from others. Wherever possible, don't move around at night – but if you absolutely have to, make sure you bring a friend to watch your back.

Cities are often the most dangerous places to be in times of disaster – there are lots of people, meaning that food and water will quickly run out. This will leave people fighting over the last few **RESOURCES** that are left. With no street lights to help people see, you never know what might be around the next corner or down the next alleyway.

With no electricity to heat or light houses, people will have to rely on fires to stay cosy in the cold winter months. While lighting a fire is a good idea, you've got to be careful – lighting fires can be dangerous and could lead to disaster if they are lit in the wrong place. Even if you're careful about where you light your fires, other people might not be. A world without power could soon lead to a world set on fire. This is another reason to stay out of the cities – where there's more people lighting fires, there's more chance for things to go wrong.

Top Tip: To stop fires from spreading, always build a circle of stones around the base of your fire. Also, have water or sand nearby so that you can EXTINGUISH the flames.

CHOOSING YOUR HIDEOUT

The perfect hideout is one that has lots of food, is well protected and is perfectly hidden from anyone who wants to get their hands on your resources. In films, such hideouts often include **ABANDONED** military bases or secret basements behind revolving bookcases. In reality, however, this type of base will be hard to find. Instead, follow these steps and you should be able to spot the perfect hideout when you come across it.

FARMLAND AND FARMING

The perfect hideout will have places for you to grow food and plenty of room for everyone that has come with you. If you can find a friendly farmer who will let you stay on his farm, that's perfect. Otherwise, look for a house just outside of a city with plenty of fields around.

The food you have in your cupboards when the power goes out will not keep you fed for long. Even if you brought lots of snacks with you as you searched for your perfect hideout, pretty soon these will run out. You're going to need to start growing your own food. You may not know anything about farming yet, but you will have to learn quickly. When you're looking for food, make sure to pick up any seeds you can and always save the seeds from fruits and vegetables, as you can plant these later.

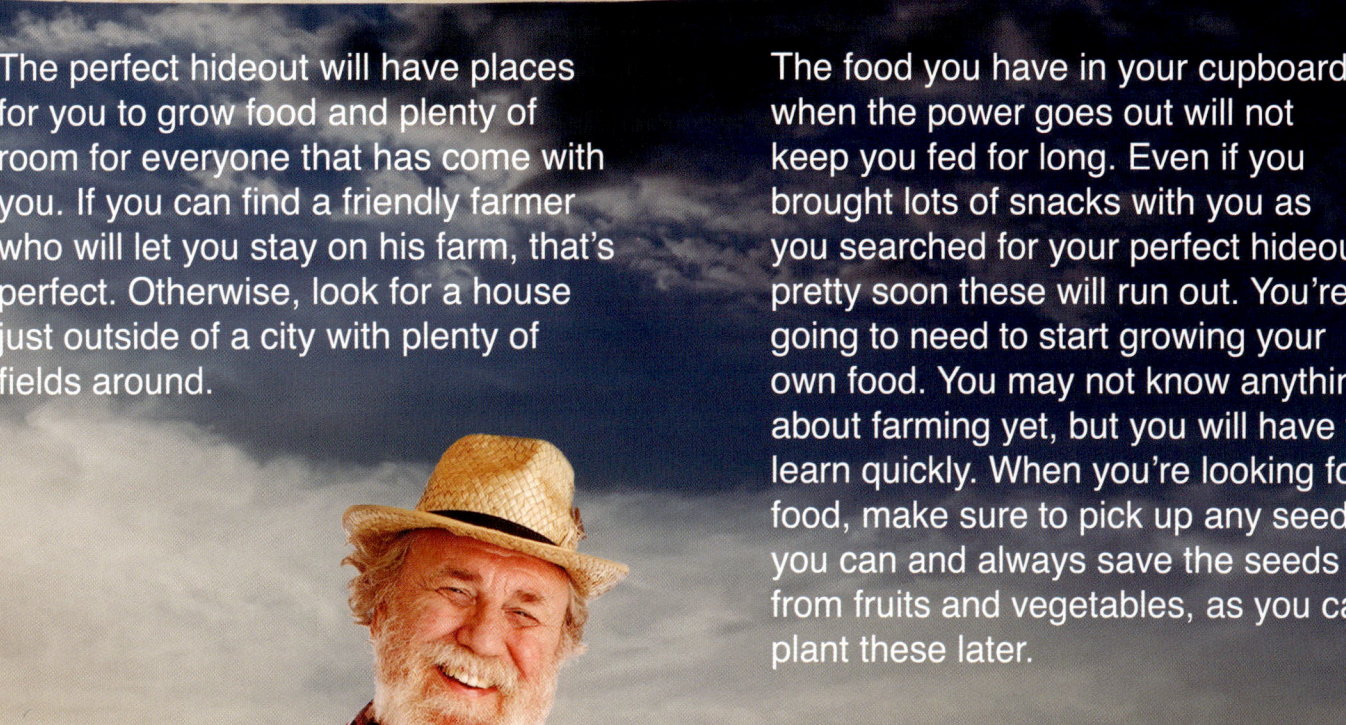

Top Tip: You can't be too picky. You'll find that you are pleased with whatever food is on the table – even Brussels sprouts!

NO MORE SHOWERS

After meeting your friends and family and getting out of the city, you are going to be tired, thirsty and probably a little smelly. Without power, the water coming out of the tap will soon be shut off. You're going to need a source of clean water to drink, wash in and water your plants with. You may not be able to have warm baths anymore, but if you can find a hideout near to a river, your life will be a lot easier.

With no **ARTIFICIAL** sources of light or heat, a fire is the best way to cook food and stay warm. While a campfire might give away your location to other people, it is worth it to stay warm and well fed. If you can, make your base near a forest so that you always have a large pile of firewood to keep your fire going.

PROTECTING YOUR BASE

It is best to work together with other people to grow food and protect your hideout. However, not everyone will be so happy to team up. Once you've established your base, other people may try and get their hands on the food and supplies you have worked so hard to gather. To defend your base, put up a fence around the area you are farming and come up with a secret PASSWORD so that only people you know can come in and out.

GATHERING SUPPLIES

Once you've found a base, you're going to need to explore the nearby area to find things that could be useful. Shops and **PHARMACIES** will soon run out of food and medicine, so you're going to need to know how to collect supplies yourself.

FOOD

When looking for food, remember that refrigerators will no longer work. Therefore, it's best to steer clear of items that will go off quickly, such as fresh meat and dairy products. After a few days, these foods will look, smell and taste horrible. Instead, start **STOCKPILING** foods that will last a long time – dried pasta, rice, oats and canned foods are the best things to go for.

> **Top Tip:** Sugar is known as a 'forever food' – a food that never goes off. While you can't live on sweets alone, sugary foods are a great thing to stockpile as they will always be good to eat.

MEDICINE

With no lights, it's only a matter of time before you trip over something and injure yourself. Medical supplies, such as bandages and plasters, will be important to make sure cuts and bruises don't get **INFECTED**. While you shouldn't take any medicine that you don't recognise, bandages and plasters are easy to use and will help to keep you and your loved ones healthy.

BATTERIES

There are some types of power that don't use mains electricity. These types of power will still work even after the electrical grid goes down. Batteries won't last forever, but in an emergency, flashlights, **WALKIE-TALKIES** and other battery-powered items will still work. Make sure to pick up batteries if you come across them – they may just save your life.

RECHARGE BY HAND

There are a number of devices that can be charged simply by winding them up. The most common items that can be charged by hand are torches and radios. If you see either a torch or radio with a handle sticking out of the side, you may well be able to charge it by hand. So grab it quickly.

Top Tip: Hand-charged radios are a great way to listen for news after the world loses its power.

PETROL POWER

Petrol can also be used to make electricity – as long as you have a generator. A generator is a small engine that burns petrol and turns it into electricity. The amount of energy a generator makes depends on how big it is. Generators should be used to make sure that the most important electrical items – such as radios and phones – stay on, even when the electrical grid is down.

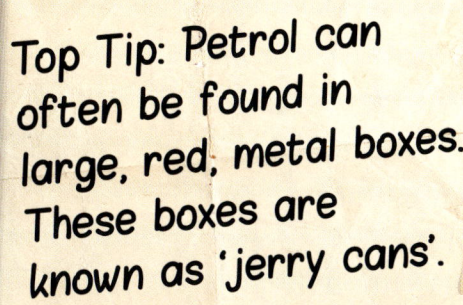

Top Tip: Petrol can often be found in large, red, metal boxes. These boxes are known as 'jerry cans'.

LIFE WITHOUT POWER

You may think that it will be impossible to live without power and all of the useful things it lets us do. However, only a tiny amount of human history has been spent with electrical power. Some of the most successful **SOCIETIES** were built without using any electricity at all. The Roman Empire, the knights of medieval England and the Egyptian pharaohs all existed before people used electricity.

Fact: The electric lightbulb is less than 150 years old. Before that, candles, oil lamps, fires and the Sun were the only sources of light.

1.2 billion people around the world still live without electricity. If they can do it, so can you!

MAKING YOUR OWN ELECTRICITY

There are lessons that you can learn from the people who have lived without electricity. People in the past came up with some clever ways to make power without plugging in to the grid. You now have the chance to put these methods to good use.

WATERWHEELS

Waterwheels are one of the oldest sources of energy. They rely on the flow of river water to make power. Waterwheels look a little bit like a Ferris wheel at a fairground, except instead of the little **CARRIAGES** where you sit, there are planks of wood. The waterwheel sits partly in the river. The water pushes the planks, which causes the waterwheel to spin.

The water wheel makes power in exactly the same way as a wind up torch or radio. The only difference is that you can lay back and relax, letting the river do all the work. While a waterwheel may not be able to charge your phone straight away, if you're clever, you can hook it up to a generator. This could eventually make enough power to light up a room, keep a refrigerator running or even power your videogames.

WINDMILLS

One of the simplest ways to make electricity is by using the wind. Windmills work exactly like waterwheels, except that instead of using water to turn the wheel, they use wind. Throughout history, windmills have been used to grind wheat to make bread. If you have been lucky enough to find a hideout with a windmill, you could attach this to your generator, just like the waterwheel, and get your fridge up and running. Then you will have somewhere to store all the food you have been busy growing! If you have grown any wheat, you could also use the windmill to make flour. Then you can make bread too!

SOLAR POWER

The biggest source of energy that we have is the Sun. The Sun gives out a huge amount of energy, heating the planet and giving plants the energy they need to grow. So far, our best way of making use of the Sun's energy is using solar panels. Solar panels catch sunlight and **CONVERT** it into electrical energy. With a large number of solar panels, you should be able to collect enough energy to power everything you need. With a working TV, an icy cold fridge and a bubbling Jacuzzi, solar panels could turn your hideout into a paradise.

Fact: More energy from the Sun hits the Earth in one day than you could use in a lifetime.

SURVIVING IN A WORLD WITHOUT POWER

If you take all the handy tips in this guide on board, then not only will you survive, but you will build an exciting new life for you and your family in the world without power. Once you're growing food and making your own energy, take the time to relax, play games, tell jokes and enjoy yourself – it may be end of life as we know it but it's not the end of the world just yet. People will want to come and join you once they see how prepared you are, so it will be your job to pass on your new-found knowledge. You could even lend them this book!

Little by little, people will learn how to rebuild the world. We did it once, so we can do it again. If you're lucky, you may even get to see the end of that movie that you were watching before the power went out!

GLOSSARY

ABANDONED — a building that no one uses or lives in any more

ADVANTAGE — to be in a better position than someone else

ARTIFICIAL — something that is man-made

CARRIAGES — an area where people sit when they are moved from one place to another

CONVERT — to change something from one form to another

DESTRUCTION — the process of damaging something so much that it is totally broken

EXTINGUISH — to put out a fire

INFECTED — a cut that has become diseased

MAGNETIC ENERGY — a type of energy that affects electrical devices and can cause them to fail

PASSWORD — a secret word used to gain entry somewhere

PHARMACIES — shops that sell medical supplies

PYLONS — a tower that is used to carry electrical wires high above the ground

REFRIGERATORS — a box, or room, which is kept cool using ice or coolant, and used to store food and drink

RESOURCES — useful items that are needed for a group to survive

SATELLITES — a man-made object in space that goes around the earth to collect information or help with communication

SOCIETIES — groups of people living together and interacting with each other

SOLAR FLARE — a short, powerful explosion of energy from the surface of the Sun

STOCKPILING — the act of saving a supply of materials

SURGE — a sudden and very strong increase

TRIBES — groups of people linked together by family, society, religion or community

WALKIE-TALKIES — battery powered radios that can be used to communicate over short distances

INDEX

batteries 22
candles 24
cities 14-15, 17-18
dangers 4, 6, 12, 14-15
Egyptian pharaohs 24
evil geniuses 5-7, 11
Electromagnetic Pulse (EMP) 6
family 10, 13, 18
farms 17, 19, 25
fences 19
fires 12, 14-15, 18, 24
food 14, 16-20, 28
generators 23, 27-28
hacking 8
heroes 4, 14
hideouts 16-19, 28-29
medicine 20-21
Native Americans 12
oil lamps 24

protection 16, 19
petrol 23
pylons 9
rebuilding 30
recharging 22
Romans 24
satellites 11
smoke signals 12
solar flares 7, 11
solar panels 29
telephones 11-12, 23
televisions (TVs) 5, 29
water 14-15, 18, 26-28
waterwheels 26-28
weapons 6
wind-up (torch, radio) 22, 27
windmills 28
wires 9

Photocredits: Abbreviations: l–left, r–right, b–bottom, t–top, c–centre, m–middle. Images are courtesy of Shutterstock.com. With thanks to Getty Images, Thinkstock Photo and iStockphoto. Cover: bg – Nik Merkulov; hands – Alex Malikov; book – Leszek Glasner. 2 – Lars Hallstrom. 3 – STILLFX. 4 – Gabi Moisa. 5 – ArtStudioHouse. 6 – Giulio_Fornasar. 7 – Twin Design. 8 tr – Merkushev Vasiliy 8b – Alexander Geiger. 9 – ESB Professional. 10: t – Rakchai Duangdee, b – Africa Studio. 11 – Dylan Law. 12 – LunarVogel. 13 – Roobcio. 14 – solarseven. 15 – fotorince. 16 – keellla. 17 bg – Mykola Mazuryk 17bl – Jeanne McRight. 18t – MRS. NUCH SRIBUANOY, 18b – Alexandr Shevchenko. 19: tl – NIPAPORN PANYACHAROEN; tr – Alex Staroseltsev; tm – Ruslan Ivantsov; m – MAHATHIR MOHD YASIN. 19 – Lpuddori. 20bg – victoras, 20br – Marcos Mesa Sam Wordley. 21bg – Billion Photos, 21tl – ROZHKOV YURIY. 22t – maerzkind, 22b – dcwcreations. 23t – Lisa F. Young, 23b – Stocksnapper. 24bg – mythja, 24br – Burlingham . 25 – R.M. Nunes. 26bg – Tithi Luadthong, 26bl – cowardlion. 27bg – jolly_photo, 27c – YK, 27m – Angyalosi Beata, 27cl – Nadezhda Bolotina, 27cb – Margo Harrison, 27br – AFH . 28 – Alexander Tolstykh. 29bg – Kajano, 29bl – espies , 29br – The Magical Lab . 30 – Monkey Business Images.